SIX FISH IN A MIX

**Alexandra Behr
and Shirleyann Costigan
Illustrated with photographs**

HAMPTON-BROWN

fin

gills

Six fish in a mix.
All have fins and gills.

Can you pick out the sawfish?

gills

fin

Six fish in a mix.
All have fins and gills.

Can you pick out the needlefish?

fin

gills

Six fish in a mix.

All have fins and gills.

Can you pick out the paddlefish?

gills

fin

Six fish in a mix.
All have fins and gills.

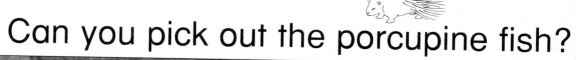

Can you pick out the porcupine fish?

 fish

 fish

 a fish

 fish

Six fish in a mix.

All have fins and gills—just like all fish.